A THOUSAND DOORS

p
o
e
m
s

b
y

Matt Pasca

Library of Congress Cataloging-in-Publication Data

Pasca, Matt.
  A thousand doors : poems / by Matt Pasca.
    p. cm.
  ISBN 978-0-9845681-6-1 (pbk.)
  I. Title.
  PS3616.A789T47 2011
  811'.6--dc22

                              2011010170

This book is a work of fiction. The characters, incidents, and dialogues are products of the author's imagination and are not to be construed as real. Any resemblance to actual events or persons, living or dead, is entirely coincidental.

20110316
JB Stillwater Publishing

20110408
Printed in the United States of America

for Terri, who makes anything possible

The Story

The title of this collection was inspired by a Buddhist parable about a poor woman named Kisa Gotami whose overwhelming joy at having birthed a son turned to crushing grief when the boy suddenly took ill and died. Crazed with sorrow, Kisa Gotami pleaded with everyone she saw to help bring the boy back to life. A kind man directed her to the Buddha, who, she was told, might have the medicine she so frantically sought. Kisa Gotami rushed to the Buddha's monastery. "Here you will find the help you need," said the Buddha, "but first you must do something for me. You must return to the city from which you just came, find me a single mustard seed and bring it back." Kisa's face lit up. "Most importantly," continued the Buddha, "the seed must come from a family in which no one has died." Kisa Gotami rushed back to her town, stopped at the first house and knocked at the door. An old woman answered. She eagerly gave Kisa Gotami a mustard seed—all India used them in cooking. But just as the seed was placed in Kisa's palm, she remembered the Buddha's stipulation. The old woman's head lowered. "I'm sorry to say the answer is yes. My dear husband died six months ago." "I am so sorry," said Kisa. "Thank you for your kindness, but I cannot take this seed." Minutes later, she knocked at the door of another house where a young woman saw Kisa standing in the doorway and came to greet her. "Can I help you?" she asked. "I am looking for a single mustard seed from a household in which no one has died," explained Kisa. "We cannot help you. I am sorry. We lost our mother two years ago," stated the young woman, quietly. "For many months I was so unhappy I didn't know how to go on, but I knew I had to help my father take care of my brothers and sisters. That's what my mother would have wanted." Kisa Gotami continued to the next house, and then to another, but always someone had lost a beloved—a brother or sister, a grandparent, an aunt or cousin, a mother or father. After a time, nightfall came. Kisa Gotami sat down, rested against a tree and felt a gradual change in herself. Not a single household she had visited lived untouched by death. Many suffered just as she did now. She was not alone. Somehow, with these thoughts, her grief lightened a bit and she returned home. The next day, Kisa Gotami readied her son for his funeral, tears streaming down her cheeks as she said farewell. Afterwards, Kisa Gotami returned to the monastery to speak with the Buddha, who saw the change in her face. He asked, "Did you bring me a tiny grain of mustard?" "No, teacher. I am done looking for the mustard seed. I know that in the whole city, in the whole world, there is not one person free from the certainty of death and suffering. At last I have said goodbye to my son. I felt terribly alone in my grief, but now I know there are many others who have lost what they most cherished. We must help each other, as you have helped me."

Contents

THANKING THE BUDDHA

THE BUDDHA'S TEST

Call to Prayer

We had just rolled our enchanted eyes—
eggplant and baklava under moonlight—
when it began: a siren
low then launching over
rooftops, splitting sapphire
above the Sea of Marmara,
a masculine echo quivering
in quarter tones, amplified
song of obedience to God soaring
from bullhorns clipped to lissome
towers on sides of mosques, our hearts
swollen like domes, our love
dancing slow and soulful
to this ballad of minarets.

E-Train Blues

Squalid stairs to platform A engulfed
in heat, air wringing throats, stifling
subway, westbound fever.

Brakes piercing rails, one
thousand bones rubbed on
bones rubbed on bones. We are
going to Manhattan to dodge
smoke and spit, tourists
whose names we'll never know.

Rocked through caverns
of desolate bulbs, aerosol
tags under river.
And the train conductor says
Next stop is Lexington,
and the train conductor says
The air conditioning is broken,
and the train conductor says
No one gives their seat to a pregnant woman!
It is 10am, and you are lost
and found in New York City.

And the train conductor says
Today's terror alert is the color of pumpkin pie,
and the train conductor says
Forty-two languages are being spoken in car 3965.
We are hurtling towards bedrock
below Manhattan.
It is 10am, and you are lost
and found in New York City.

Gone rabid for homeless, for museums
with subsidized fees and international renown.
Gone rabid for bodacious taxis
and microcosms, New York beckons
artists to come to her in the morning,
in the evening, at midnight,
on time; the city loves time.

Tanyou

Above taxi queues, gift shops, red velvet
loops and black CB's—The Metropolitan,
second floor, Manhattan; bamboo and trickles
pool below tiered eaves of a Ming pagoda,
home to winged moonlight and reluctant
spirits falling still.

In this Suzhou scholar's retreat, I am lifted
by the blue arms of heaven, as in summer
when breeze and constellation rock us to sleep—
restless eyes called to dream of gardens and balance:
boulder and stream, pain and peace.

We are an Eastern species
choking on Western ideals:
Compete! Achieve! Consume!

But Shiva dances on a lotus, Nataraj
creating and destroying by fire; His hand
gestures *Do not be afraid.* There
is Buddha, folded in our sun-warmed core,
urging us to detach. And there are temples,
facades of camphor and gingko
fashioned by reverent hands to welcome
us from centuries we have outrun
answering a shrill, misguided bell.

Listen
to the drip of melting ice,
the bullfrog at water's edge,
crickets in the hot night,
the lowing of mottled cows,
the swish of maple leaves,
the silence of the stones.

Listen to your own ancient
drum, thumping its way towards infinity.

The Oldest Story

for Brian

I just want to kill things
you grinned as you leaned
in my classroom doorway
the day you enlisted.
But I knew
it was your father
you meant, not the Fallujans.

Third period Myth class,
you sat: six-foot-four, marble-eyed lineman
hulking over the flat square
of desk in your hands. Through you
discussions swooned, punctured by
your laughter, unabashed
viewpoints and whimsical
passion for cheesecake.

For midterm, you performed
The Epic of Gilgamesh in toga, sash and sandals,
breathing life into cuneiform tablets—
an arrogant Demigod, cursed
with a need for immortality. You deployed

last month for a second
tour of Iraq—
land of Gilgamesh and Eden—
the sweet sauce of our class
dried and bitter
in your sandworn throat.

Screams now split
your sleep, invoking dad's
old taunts and tyrannies
as you realize, like Gilgamesh,
you set out to vanquish
a mirage.

At home
we want you back

but know you
won't be whole.

You are a Demigod too dark
for cheesecake, too wise for laughter—
like your Sumerian King,
humbled so long ago
by knowledge he was
never meant to have.

Passing It On

You snapped her
Polaroid by the red maple—
your curbside daisy:
pigtails, white dress, thumbing
bark as she posed,
a conduit of light.

You kept close watch on
barbecue Sundays, pacing
the perfect rectangle, grass
prickling at your shoe-tops,
paper plates, cold cuts
and sweets for Lenny's precinct pals.

But day to day, thinking
husband safe
enough, you did not
consider what he taught her
on evening walks to Krausers
while you ran errands,
or when his monstrous feet splintered
floorboards at midnight.

Your little girl, stretched
by the maple, supine
down the hall, hiding
in the attic of her skull
like her mother—
your bodies
still with absence.

Had you stood, stopped
him, your own secret
might have risen—a dark weed
poking through the concrete of night—
and been used to make his
crime your fault.

Still a conduit
of light, she forgives
and blazes for you now:
You reach like ivy,
as if to curl under
doorframes, over mattresses,
down New Brunswick sidewalks
to snap her back from the man
you never wanted.

Your hands are not
as long as you'd like—
your sorry never big
enough to put your shame
to sleep.

On Your 36th Birthday

It was almost midnight when
you asked from the indigo,
eyes constellations
above the floating hull
of my body: *Write about this—*
that will be my present.

When I start to think of our moments
they expand, like rice in water.

We fly miles above our pasts
spent sifting through closetlands,
grasping for some wide cotton
world to fall into. God is in this
bond, whether we believe in God or not.
Our son yawns and lays his hand on your arm.

I could never map all the streets of our city.

We are oceanside in the morning,
the dark sand our only witness.
Others play in our afternoon waves
but can never know
how deep this goes, how far
beyond the eye, how each
hour I cannot be with you
my heart is a wide hangar waiting
for the flight of you
to arrive.

In Lieu of Narnia

Evening crowds in and rage blasts through
our house, unhinging doors, belching
lava in violent crescendos: father and brother—
twin volcanoes blown; mother and I—seas
recessed and reddened.

There is nothing to do but wince
as words erupt, lip to lip, singeing paint
with cinders, echoes splitting streetside
oaks and crashing neighbors' porch-lights till they fall,
submerged in the swamp-high shame of our yard.

My father hobbles forward, a hydra
of ego and despair, curses cracking like wind
across a torn and flapping sail; my mother mists
a vapor too thin to protect.

On the smoldering staircase in Pittsburgh Steelers pajamas—
maize polyester itching thighs—I hope
my presence will make it stop, make it quiet,
make it all go away. But heat has me fumbling
for my bedroom door, swung wide, shut up,
their voices a thousand chainsaws rising
through the flesh of my brain. There is no wardrobe
in my sky blue room to walk through, no snow-licked
lamppost or Mr. Tumnus, no lion to whisk me away.

So I leave:
starboard edge of mattress, staring flat-line
staring frozen through the wall—adrenaline
and bone with a trampoline heart, prone
in a Star Wars-curtained courtroom, no language
in my severed mind, no gavel or robe
to help me object or douse these nightly infernos
with truths I know they will remember
when the lava cools and their
pride is forgotten.

Had I stuck around to swallow
the size and sorrow of it—joined

the voices rousing nails from wooden beds,
singing sawdust into cracks where termites
cannot go—I'd have broken
like a top string tuned too far.

Hardly a boy, a rent ember
in the dark of a little house
on a little street, distended with justice
undone, affection foregone, trying to soften
in a time when volcanoes scorched the seas
and all the right words
turned to stone.

Letters

I like the rhythm of letters,
the way, for example, a cursive *q*
spins twice counterclockwise and heads
east, or how the rounding hat
of an *f* peers on tippy toes
over *g*'s fence because his grass
really is greener.

I like the friendships letters form:
ambivalent *c* and placid *h*
changing to cha cha champs
cheerfully chasing chances
and charming children who
channel chaos—
or when *p* steals off to meet *h*
at a midnight rendezvous where,
under cover of philodendron, they can
f in the dark.

Even *x*'s are excellent,
though mostly for warning—
the siren of the alphabet
alerting us to extremes,
exterminations, axes,
taxes, and *ck*'s who
want to be slang.

There's a stupor about *abc,* I think,
burdened with alphabetic representation—
in every nursery school cupboard,
on every rainbow-streaked cereal box;
is it any wonder how often
they call a *cab*, find a *k*
and go *back* home?

And I never fail
to enjoy the stealth of a *g*
or *e* or *p* that hides by a neighbor
without making a sound, hoping

to be overlooked long enough
to belong, for good.

Twenty-six worlds of sound,
doubled when they spin as thirteen
couples: serif to serif, foot to foot,
dancing harder then softer, though
none so beautifully as *u* and *i.*

This Week Had Arms

They flung open, feathers dipped from
      elbows pilling,
      curled and carmine;
they hung,
waiting to whip
      through horns of wind,
      cones of exhaust, ascending,
dreaming of Charles Lindbergh in Parisian streets.
      My week's arms stretched—
squeezed me from Milwaukee,
from Washington Heights, through the Internet—
Boo-ya!
I blushed. She said
PS, I need you want you love you, the compost
of her wisdom producing in me a blossom.

Her voice whirls and climbs in my head—a carousel
accordion jangles till my eyelids close. My body spins
against her hot, pink tongue,
the cleansing slice of her throat,
the speed of comfort in the dark,
the howl of beauty in my hands
plucking curves of elation
from graph-papered air.

My body doesn't spin really—
it rocks like a rope moored to shoreline
crashing undertow, crashing undertow
and when she speaks, I am sucked to the sea.
Hey beautiful on the tips of waves,
the melodic glass of her aura
stained orange and blue by the sky.
In this ocean of growing infinities
I am found, bobbing at once in all hemispheres.

There are no waters through which I am not permitted to swim
Потому что я ее люблю. They heave and cradle
me in their arms; the wet bulk
of the world buoys me
up, balanced and safe.

Ghosts

Holding my breath in the slate jade bi-level on Nims Avenue
to fend off smoky plaits of Kent 100's, I shrank away—
from his pink Tab-can saccharine fizz, the orange plash
of iodine smeared across his fistula, the dull stink
of saliva glistening in his thistled beard.

Elbows folded in my ears to stem
the slash of his reckless self-pity, I tracked
his savage hammer of spite as it smashed the white
aluminum front door and ricocheted
through caverns in our bones.

It wasn't always bad—sometimes dad
was really dad—but then, I wasn't me, the damage
done, heart on lockdown to thwart the tenderness
of his dark mystical smile, the sonorous
lilt of unmedicated words.

For ten years, with the only childhood
I had, I steeled myself for the coming
of his silent, unexceptional death:
November '89, hospital lounge, eighteenth floor.

My two boys
do not know I had a father before
Grandpa Harry, do not know what it's like:

to feel cheated of years,
equate speech with peril,
have to dream cool canyons of unailing love
and realize—despite whatever time is shared—
no one is really there.

Perigee

My two-year-old knew
the planets by March,
their moons by June
and in July dropped
an apple
on my head:
Isaac Newton! he cried.

We spent August at the planetarium.
He'd clutch me till Mars turned its red face
toward us—hot toddler breath, thumbs
in my collar. I'd rock him
beneath the flickering dome
through thunder and watergun raindrops.

In that synthetic squall,
eyes damp against his cheek, I'd try
to hold him well enough to shield
him from life's inexorable meteors. If only
there had been a way, then—
as close as we would ever be—
to heat the grand core of his heart
beyond capacity.

Instead, I assured his future
self in vain, my love
like a ceiling of stars
whose light stretches out
from a distant past, long
before the storms have come.

March Baseball

Our boys snap
their wrists, kick up
dust and slide headlong
beneath the purple
awning of equinox.

They smack a white pea
far and hard against
the backdrop of brown
convection domes and a basketball
court where truants perfect
their daily attendance.

Batters shift their weight, ready for
the off speed, collect momentum,
hungry for the *clink*—
pealing consonance of alloy
and horsehide.

Geometrically hemmed, this constellation
of a ball field: our center
fielder—hub of Cassiopeia's W;
the boy stealing signs from second base—
glinting notch in Orion's belt;
the first base coach—
Ursa Minor's sidelined handle.

In the slow metric orbit of a March
ball game, everyone's a star.

Redshift

The cats curl—
two apostrophes
on straight line of bed,
oblivious to the monitored static
of our son's breath
next door.

This first step:
the distance
between us
and him
inevitable,
like the sad slip
of daylight in autumn.

The loss began
when he left
the haven
of his mother's womb, where
he'd kicked in time
to her feet,
hiccupped into the taut curve
of her belly.

For her, the sure
broadcast of his breath
is but a warm slipper,
her feet bare and cold
between apostrophes.

Feet

Four sets of unlike feet. My mother's, splotched with varicose webs, are pale and sheer like tracing paper on a road map. And me, my feet are big. I mean, when I was twelve I could act my age *and* my shoe size. Jesse has jaguar feet, kind of sleek and sable—almost elegant—ready to pounce on you or steal off into silence.

But my father's feet, my father's feet, like gnarled snake-skins, all stained and scaled with diabetes, tough to look at as he sat smoking on the couch, smoking though he knew it'd kill him faster, were sprinter's feet long before his nails yellowed and horned over in taloned apostrophes, before he tripped on a clipboard and had half his right one lopped off, before they were bandaged and slathered with Betadine, before they became angry sacks of cracked dough caned through the narrow chain-link gap behind Shop Rite to the last baseball game he'd see me play, where I captained the Varsity team alone, rapping lonely doubles into alleyways, swiping lonely bases, diving for lonely line drives, shaking hands, alone, with opponents. The *chink* of the aluminum bat, the empty baselines and my father's feet that looked like cracked dough.

Gateau de Mille-Feuilles
(Cake of a Thousand Leaves)

Sometimes, my consciousness heaps dimension
upon dimension, slotting each of my former selves
beneath its successor like the almond-sweet
strata of a Napoleon:

impossible to slice,
the custard sticks
tight to stories of puff
pastry, fondant combed
dark and light, layers
mashing on contact, some sliding
out from the rest in a rush of creamy tectonics.

Identity
is a messy thing.

For Remus Lupin

I am too old for Hogwarts, can't
meet you by the Boggart closet
or covered bridge, but I want to
open your classroom door
and tell you I, too, know
the barometric dip,
weightless drop
into namelessness—
like a glorious symphony that,
upon waking, evaporates
one

        note
 at   a
   time.

It's the *No-Not-Again* moment
that hurts worst: the first sliver
of moon that turns you
to foreign husk
while you watch, aghast
and dumb.

We have lived this secret
too long, our brotherhood
of fractured men grown
accustomed to falling through
fissures without warning.

I want to grab your human
hand to say I know why
you run from Tonks, hoping
to spare the next to love you—
why you train students to repel
what can make them hollow.

Good professor, this
Patronus you teach—that shields
from non-being—is love
cast from somewhere inside
the flat-line of your heart.

It is time for us to be found
out—to risk being
needed, hungry for fullness,
fissures or not.

We must be wary
of moons, yes, but
we can be whole, human
almost always
and that, to be sure,
is enough.

Osiris Speaks to Isis

That November I died
without dying, the Nile bore me
off in a lead-sealed chest, cracked
figs and mulberries lancing
the bank as Ra's eye grew
hotter, Set's desert wider,
like his grin—only you
could have saved me.

You sped after currents,
blessed river children for pointing,
nursed princes for penance till you sniffed
my casket—cool cedar in the shade
of Damascus morning.
You plied me from palace
columns, your wings
draping my carcass
with wishes.

In a chamber of gold, you
hovered with fury, kissing
life into my shameful length.
I came to in measures, restored
by your stubborn miracles;
the Nile charged with green
and bustle, date palms, heft
of blue in bronzed fingers
that prayed to the goddess who
set right rift of sun and land:
you—who hovers in my tightening chest,
you—the gift that opens me again
and again.

Head of the Bomb Squad

Best in the biz
said the chief—
Lenny's black beret draped
over grenade
paperweight, pistol
in his buckle, broken
nose sniffing the real deal
from a fake, holes
in his bones blown
by foster fire.

His long, scarred fingers
were swift to thwart detonation
but no one in Jersey built
as many bombs in a crude cellar
below twenty-four stairs he climbed to his daughter's
bedroom—head racing with demons—
where he crammed her full
of explosives.

But if mercy is crucial,
something must be said
for my shrapnel-filled father-in-law,
dead at fifty-three:

He passed on
some tools of the trade—
just enough tenacity and wit
to help her diffuse, over decades,
the rounds he left buzzing
in her warm, white body.

Shirts and Skins

I was a cliché: the pimply teen,
acne a badge of adolescence like pubic
hair and crass jokes their tellers
don't understand.

At fourteen, my back—once soft olive
sloping through fields, flattening
teepees of dirt and grappling
with dinosaurs—erupted.

I stockpiled black tees to hide
bloodstains, pustules oozing
between mouths and backpacks
swung like meteors
from stairwells.

I spun toward voices
like a fugitive, dread trilling
my spine of tender cysts
that, if touched, could break
me open, drain me across
the tiles between gymnasiums
A and B where old men in polyester
coached us into corners.

In the locker room, my hidden
skin blood-stuck cotton,
I shunned all who might slap
my secret from me, or crack
the scab of each scream preserved
from the battlefield my brother
and father walked:

Two generals issuing gunfire
through the night, their mines
in my flesh, pending detonation.

At center court, Coach Tightshorts counted
us to ten—*evens are shirts, odds are skins.*

My fists balled white, spine
pocked and sore, feeling old,
feeling faint, trying to hold
this war together.

It's Never the Flesh

never carnal consummation
that makes it hard.

It's that his laughter by the
coffee stand still rippled your
smile as you cooked pasta
in my favorite pot.

It's never palms spread and sheets
sweating, lips left open for the sky
to fall into.

It's the way your childish frame swayed
by his doorway between lunch
and recess, hands snatching at
glue-sticks like batons.

It wasn't the way you said I should sleep
in another bed, troll the basement
of my own house—a husband underground—
unable, literally, to stand up.

And it's not the way writing
a novel about your ex, who landed
you in a mental ward, made you pine
for his corn-silk hair, and not me.

It was the way my despair,
to you, was lined with the frosting
of promise, each fallen wall
of our ruins a Triumphal Arch
where you and he could meet.

It's how you took what I thought
true and yanked it clear,
how I lost six years to your grinding
mind that tallied human complexities
like an actuary, while I paid
the bills and fed the cats.

Misplaced

I've a Hindu heart, avatars
in my blood, a spinning wheel
of fire at the breast of a village
woman whose atman sings of Moksha.

I've an indigenous soul, born of birdsong
and cockle shell, fluted clay and drumbeats
in centers of towns that are circles, as all life
is circular: the elk, the moose, the seasons,
the tides and the nests.

I've a Persian spirit, Zarathustra's son,
fighting Ahriman at your side, O Kind Lord,
Avestan on my tongue, your seven angels
of good mind my closest friends.

I've a body of mystery,
from Mayan ziggurats to Chilean Moai,
Zen gardens to Uluru—each
feeling more like myself
than email, pay stubs
and the family name.

Natalie, Who

Posed on a black and white Mount Vernon sidewalk in 1945, face taut, coat pressed; walked miles to the opera house with her Phebo; strolled home hand in hand, two Gods of the Proletariat, smiling in the wake of an aria; fed two crow-haired boys the milk of words and knowledge; chuckled at the way my father said *Egypt-i-an* when he was a child; bought him a hammer and army-issue sack for hunting rocks by roadsides; bought and sold Long Island houses for pastime and profit; spackled, grouted, stripped carpets and rolled decades of walls with forearms flecked with paint; fried two oily hot dogs in her floral Lindenhurst kitchen just the way I liked them; who, with legs bowed like parentheses, stood at her daughter-in-law's stove—the one with the microwave built into the top—mating spatulas and slotted spoons with casserole pans and colanders; whose meals made me love holidays I did not celebrate; who hemmed the passing years with enchanted aromas but never sat down to eat; mastered arancini and ziti and slip-covered furniture despite not being Italian; who, in silk Asian blouses and gold pendants, sat on a wooden folding chair by the stairwell Christmas Eve, black Hefty hoop between her knees for wrapping paper jump shots; was never fooled by slick politicians or the rhetoric of injustice; sat across from you at the table when no one else was around, eyes dilated by spectacles, listening with the orderly attention of the cosmos; who *tssked* and said *Isn't that something* when awed by the world; said *clever, darling* and *keeping company*; folded her top lip over the bottom one when touched with glee or girlish mischief; dazzled with pristine wisdom and a low brassy voice, both preserved beneath the shale of Sicilian patriarchy; who deflected praise like a bulletproof tank; slipped like sand from the other end of the phone; who lost a son and husband in one year but chose to live and grow; who never stopped learning; didn't think everything new was a step backwards; who sometimes channeled Bill Moyers; once traveled five hours to hear me sing; who, cheeks flexed into jowls, sliced cake with graceful serration, her husband's lion ring roaring over butter cream roses; who broke her hip at eighty-four and worked a 40-hour week two months later; hair streaked white and taupe, knuckles polished and swollen, sorted stamps for my uncle with expert care; who laughed with the full force of her being; filled me with pride and adoration; taught me the power of humility, service and language; who passed quietly in a back room of Kodak-covered bureaus at ninety-four, her lips circled in awe, as if to say *Isn't that something*; and who, on the gurney under maroon fleece, seemed so much longer than her four-foot-ten-inch frame, restored perhaps to her original height. Natalie, my grandmother, who always leaned up, way up when we met—as far as she could go—to plant a wet full-lipped kiss on my cheek.

Ode to NPR

How is it I never anticipate
the bearing of the trees?
Green softens sightlines,
sings to the air
so long it takes root in
welcome lungs.

Then one day, I am behind
the wheel: gaunt groves
snarl with javelin teeth and desolation
blankets the brittle road with ice. I gasp,
growing uncertain of certainties.

It is then
the air-thin alto of soccer moms—
some white, some Mexican—
on the bleachers of a ravaged North Carolina town
cheer together for their children;
and tears prick at Ric O'Barry's voice,
his Hollywood dolphin past tied
to their September slaughter in Taiji;
and Steve Inskeep reports that variations of biryani and pilau
are remarkably slight along the Grand Trunk Road
between Peshawar and Kolkata;

And it is then
the ice beneath my wheels
thaws, complexity sprouts,
and I remember myself—
and the green that keeps me whole.

A Thank You to William Bayard Cutting

His Tudor mansion commands the hill, green
mile of tongue to the Connetquot—
land chiseled, coin of Reconstruction rails,
ferry and sugar beet, pruned and left to us.

We sneak through the hissing
sanctum of oak, sassafras, pitch pine and holly,
Wonderlands to flit through, blood
softened, steps slowed to the pace
of petal and stalk. A weeping beech twists
us through centuries of intimate incisions
while knees of bald cypress break
the skin of a riverbank.

In the chlorophyll core of my pupil, white rectangles
alight with the plastic sheen of rhododendron; yellow
carnations chunk like the secret meat
of an apple; a lone street gulch shadows
trail three, its rows of stones bound in igneous
parity; a queue of goslings scoots and bobs
along the surface of a pond—striders dart deftly
in between—and snappers dig ditches for their young.

There is sibilance of water and leaf,
aping the rhythm of earthly circuit,
and in the slow-motion shade an alliance of lindens reaches
until lit, as do we, in darkness.

Crossing paths with strangers
who smile, we are warmed like flora
by the sun, our roots meeting
in the womb of a tycoon's arboretum—
learning together beneath the
skyful eye of God.

Thoughts of an Almost Dad

Sometimes when Farsi spirals
in soprano supplication, choirs recline
to belt gospel through the roof
or willow braids swing through the hoop
of sunlight above my head, I feel,
for a solitary second,
I am your equal.

When God peeks through
holes of mortal vision,
I can imagine your soul—
how beautiful you are
already, untouched
by the coarse debris
of human shores.

Between worlds:
a matrix of stardust
where all is wet and fecund—
Eden within your mother—
a month yet from the cold
sudden lash of wind,
whirr of turning earth.

These are cosmic days,
ripening toward a present
I never imagined for myself:
so long fortressing, noting marvels
with pen and paper, safe and detached—
just a film now flashing
past the storefront of my mind.

I am awed
by what I stand to gain:
my heart ringing like a bell
when you smile
or search flowerbeds for the bee—
my empty hands soon
filled with miracles.

The Blow

My brother never forgave my mother
for letting dad steer his eleven-year-old
fingertips across the surface of a Ouija Board
and tell their eager son he'd been
a rapist and murderer in a past life.
He slammed her sweet
advances shut, her pleas gathering
like motes in the shining
beam of his anger.

When I was fifteen, he loomed
over her sagging figure in rose
shadows of cheap curtains,
beating her down
with his mouth.
Finally off my bed,
I walked down the stairs
and stood in the stunned air
between perfume and violence.

*If you don't move
I'll hit you*, he said, but
it had taken me ten years
to reach that small patch
of rug between them.
He punched me in the jaw
and I knew his knuckles
were kinder than the hands
that fought demons
behind the door my mother
seemed so bent on opening.

Permit and keys, I drove
bridge to beach, the imprint
on my cheek lit gold by sunset over Great South Bay.
On the other side I broke down—
my car had stopped. The police officer looked surprised
when a decade of tears spattered
the hood of my hot, listless engine.
It's ok, he said, *we'll get you home.*

Halfway

between chipped limestone and whipped-cream
contrails that stripe high summer skies,
tight-cropped knolls of estates and splintered
shacks at the end of Moffitt Lane:
a point that is neither
and both.

How am I to know
when I am halfway
between instructor and
dad, friend and
husband, citizen and
soul? What is the vertex of that line
attending me from mammal
to poet, boy to
man, coward to
hero? How far from those laminate-paneled years
in house number fifty-seven must I run
to be halfway beyond the haunted
grove of childhood?

I would so love to know
when I am halfway done becoming
a good person, when I might put a bookmark
in my life, sit for a bit, and plan out
Act Two like a vacation.

KNOCKING ON DOORS

Grace

The trick is to like heartache
but not too much.

It is good to feel
the wince of April
dogwoods—pink and rousing
before June, or to bask in your son's
unmitigated smile, knowing
mitigations will come.

But it is not good to seek
what simply will break
you, like a compelling
lover who cannot give
you what you need, or
a baseball team that
will never win.

It is good, though, to embrace
eighteen-year-olds setting out
for their Ithakas, knowing
you, their teacher, will be left
back again, or to let your lips
linger on the mouth
of a woman with whom
conversation carves an atlas
of roads across your face
before leaving her again.

But it is certainly not good to forget
God, and by that I mean all
that you have learned: the ocean
wind that blows cold
yet holds you, changed
butterflies beating into thick
canopies of light, the sacrament
of song and dance that gives
voice to grief.

The trick is to like heartache
just enough to convert it
to wonder and let it move
you the way all the embers of galaxies spin
away from that single source
in silent, parallel flight.

Grabbing At Water

On this scree of Berkshire limestone
by Wahconah Falls, I form a *t* with my legs
and write to you, little man, not quite
a year, asleep in your mother's arms.

You have brought us to New England—
land of foliage and quiet glinting—
because by Lefferts Laundromat, you arch
back your head—clouds in your throat—
point up at branches and like a thousand
unleashed swallows cry *ooooOOOOOoooo*
into the Queens afternoon.

This morning, out the side window
of our rental, acrylic streaks of roadside danced
red and gold across your watchful
cheeks: tumbling gravestones, pumpkin
farms, scarlet avenues and cedar shutters all singing
of autumn, of home, of seeking.

I sit near white lattice pouring
into pools of light filtered in
through slimming treetops—and consider the spring
of light within you, from which
you draw each day, how we lean
like birches as you shine
from place to place.

And when you wake
I know you will reach for the plummeting
static of the falls, desperate
to clutch its strident charge,
hold it in time so
you won't forget. Like these words
are all I have.

Silence

When hearts swell or crack
there are no words—
words are not
life, but keep us alive
when we are not living.

Why is it
we speak so much?

I have never looked at a cricket
without knowing it was a cricket,
yet the experience is not *cricket.*

Without words we see
lichen, jetties, the cold glare
in city windows; we mend
rips and tears; we hear
the concert of sparrows; we
finger the rim of beauty.

You and I might meet and sway
like two branches in
a breeze, our skins
completing each other's
landscape, only jagged
breath to puncture rhythm.

My eyes and fingers you may read,
and if you slow down and listen
you will hear yourself inside
of me, blowing like a hundred
leaves on a forest trail.

And if I move while you are not
looking do not ask why:
there are peat mounds and brambles
that will know where I have gone.

Estuary

for Harriet Pasca-Ortgies

At times I over-
flow, sweep into white-capped
teeth of ocean. Peace
stutters and reels—and she comes,
from a thin, brackish
loch of tidewater,
speaking lost
words with an ancient
tongue, guiding
me to land.

Narrowsburg, NY

Freshwater dreams:
a Fisher Price shovel,
twig bridges for ants,
tadpoles on the tops
of your river shoes,
near a bench
that stares into the face
of a rye field—
Delaware River Country,
and not a sound
to make you think
otherwise, or care at all
what it's called.

Put your mind in a canoe
and let the current take it.
I'll slice the pie, shuck
the corn and sing the virtues
of evening.

Night Owl

Filaments buzzed in the light
above the ochre stairwell
between my brother's room and mine.
The coast had cleared: splintering
door jambs, crashing plates and words—
like tridents—stirring puddles into floods.

Just one bulb,
dangling, as my family
of tired warriors dropped
their shields and went to bed.
In the small, brave glare I
emerged—an orphan bulb
buzzing where no one could find
it, unscrew it, or make it dark.

I was a night owl, sprung
safe and free from its hole, in love
with night, when my animal
self could fly over the cramped, concrete
limb of Nims Avenue—year after year
like an anxious lover, ear pressed
to the chest of nightfall's vibrant solitude,
soaring towards sunrise.

But life lightened: I learned to participate
in daylight, roughhouse with two sun-haired
boys and share afternoons with a wife
who tenders the fullest embrace. I came to
greet the morning sun and dawning
of quiet gratitude that ensures the coming day
won't knock me over like a pin.

And now, through the dark
mouth of hours that once bled
my voice, I sleep the soundest
of sleeps, lights all turned off,
their filaments fit
only for dreams.

Mako Sica

Today, I watch the weather sipping
from an olive canteen. My thirst releases, a cold
front juts over the Badlands horizon: its sky, like
my love, is indigo.

To the east, past interludes of white spiraling
vapor is another, more brutal storm, scowling pitch and jagged
electric, cracking thumbtacks into the plain.

Above this prairie where wind and water have chiseled
mesas into spires, my defenses erode, and I think of you, Jesse.
Ours was an impossible choice: become brothers or survive.
I hid away, mixing salves of peace in my blue bedroom
while you Ghost Danced on plateaus, bellowing deep
and restless for the wounds of the world, unstitched
in your dogged heart.

Now I smile at your spinning
epiphanies, how you've again touched some ineffable thumping,
sparking orange in your eye like the sea
waves at sundown back home. You rise and fall
and repeat, but have always known to love.

Among these Lakotan pinnacles, watching
cumulonimbus from afar, my canteen is empty
but I am wet with admiration, brother,
for your unceasing soul: as bold, sad
and magnificent as the stain
of the rain in this indigo.

Orchard

I am shirtless under porch light, ox-bow
vein coiled in my bicep, blue flicker of TV
dancing coolly in the trees down Ridgeway Boulevard.
Peach pit in my left hand, poised for tossing
into black can for Friday pickup. The pit
is pock-marked, withered red, blood
drained into my palm, and I remember
being eight:

A quiet hugging boy, roving
through hours between solitude
and fear, among sheaves of mica and rotting
blackberries—the moment asked little
of me. I tossed my pit high and hard,
its juice staining my knuckles while it sailed
over wiffle field, blackberry bush
and clothesline into the garden, where
in April, my mother found
a small peach tree. She replanted it
behind the deck where it grew to maturity.

On this late night stoop, crickets
humming, leaves flashing blue, I wonder
what would happen if I tossed this pit
over my shoulder,
over this darkened street
and into the sky—
my life already seeming
an elegant chain of accidents.

The Payoff

In Bohemian circumference we sat
under cherry blossom, in front of the school—
fifty brown, pale or panty-hosed legs
cross-hatched by grass and pressure,
pens scrawling in windless blue afternoon.

Sunlight lifted us in shafts
of possibility; but for the rank carburetor groan
of long yellow buses, all was perfect.

I looked around the circle
at my twenty-five young friends, writing,
and felt there was nothing more
I could have done to arrive
at this blooming oneness.

The world fell soft and open
before me that day, collecting my heart
with forgiving hands.

In Praise of Exposure

Salt and pepper ash puffed across my parents'
bedwall, their drawers half open, strewn
with single socks, cigarette lighters and hard
candies, glossy mags beneath Dad's dresser.

He sat, burning orange and tin by kerosene,
McNeil-Lehrer trumpeting on Channel 13, his twisted
fingers listing mineral species in a red
pharmacy notebook, my mother
in black leotard, my father
in Velcro and velour, my brother
in and out of Camaros
and Italian doorways of glass
and mocha, raging.

Clumps of algae stuck to the sides
of our tank, keyholes of gossamer
green through which mollies, gouramis
turned away without pretense—like mom and dad
vanished into glucometers, gauze
and emasculation.

Every night at 7:05, Mets on Channel 9,
my father in a burnished maroon
recliner, left arm hooked to a blinking
wall of machine that freed his blood
of toxins—translucent tubes and tense
levers that did what his kidneys
could not. He rooted Mookie, Doc
and The Kid on as I leaned by the door,
hopeful and scared.

But the truth, plainly, was death;
he would die—we would all die—
and life still could be beautiful;
wrap the ticking bombshell
of organs in a papoose—that
is how you survive; stick a fistula in your heart
filter out the shit, make it clean
and be on your way.

Truth starts out hard and gets easier.
Pretense starts out easy and lulls
you into paralysis. That I was taught
truth, not pretense
might be the only thing
that saved me.

Opening Day

Billy Knapp Field: raked clean of stone and weed,
bases gleaming white lime diamonds under clouds,
raffles, anthems, hot chocolates, and speeches—a study in Americana.

Between 2nd and 3rd, the tee-ball Reds, synthetic iron-on
steam between shoulders, my son a tall number one,
his glove attached like glue, arms like windmills, four-year-old
body a kite to be steered by Coach John. Now first pitch, politician
with scissors, board-of-directors-man yells *Play Ball!*
and it's back to the park where this parade began—
children and baseballs, cleats and helmets that sparkle
before grass-stains and scuffmarks collect.

Down Penataquit, the high firstworn hose
of four-five-six-year-olds shimmer red
under charcoal skies, flashing police lights
and bulging C's stitched on bills over noses—
primal spray of drumstick and glockenspiel
calling this suburban rite to families crouched
around fences, staked out for glimpses of innocence.

His restive fingers in mine, I say how proud
I am to be his father, ask if he liked the ceremony—
he tilts his wobbly cap, says *Yeah, I did. But two boys*
were killing a worm. I told them, 'That worm is still alive!'
His chin quivers, eyes darting from dogwood to maple
to asphalt glowing red beneath his feet, and he says—
thought unfurling like a crowded flower—*Maybe they don't like worms.*

In the car, familiar flashcards in hand, their forty-three names
like buds upon his tongue—*Jackson, Van Buren, Harrison, Tyler*—
he asks which presidents were good and which ones were bad.
I leave him to repeat his question as only four-year-olds will—undeterred.

This affords me a wistful minute to study
gardens at stop signs and fashion a phrase
to tell his smooth-shadowed face that, really, there is no good or bad—
just those who try to kill worms
and those who try to defend them.

Show and Tell

Joe Punk squashed it—
that was really his name—big feet
for a kindergartner, smile swarthy
and crooked like his hair.

Ms. Feld threatened Joe with chalk-dust
glares and ruler-smack hands;
Joe snickered and sat down.

It lay scrunched and dark
like a Groucho mustache—the caterpillar
I had found at dusk, late August,
named and told bedtime stories
for a month—now creased upwards,
now feet thrashing, now juicing into white
tabletop, straight and still
as a gymnast's leg.

I noticed it shiver, a minuscule
leafish stir against a backdrop of cots
and faces that gawked, waiting
to see if I'd crumple
like my pet. Instead, something vast
and merciless, like Joe Punk's black
Converse, welled up
in my reeling
body: the revelation that
this
was how it would be.

Waffle House Blues

Give us this day our daily bread
and eggs, hash browns and coffee
while I flip, slice and cut on a flat black
grill in a Mississippi Waffle House,
babbling to myself about Vickie's slutty friends,
Mr. Bland's beer belly and my great Aunt
Cheryl's fake emerald toilet seat.

An omelet made is an omelet earned,
mumbling to myself about my busted Hyundai,
stolen night school notebook and bedroom
window got jacked by a tree.

There's no place like this shithole,
no place like this shithole,
but clicking my sorry-ass heels
won't take me nowhere,
ranting to myself about why I'm
gonna lose it if the guy just walked in
orders a fuckin' latte.

Imagining Dubya

When I wear the red
tie and pressed pants,
creases taut, bucks
shined, I believe
what I am saying.
The folds above my cheekbones lift
and I forget
the grottos of my shame,
where memories shatter in figure
eights between orange and white
barrels on blackened roads.

In board-stiff
double-lapelled suits
I grin, shake
hands, review policies,
sip from a clear glass
and feel fit for
this job. But at night
no presidential robe can swaddle
my conscience; these
demons persist, caged
above boxwood and portico.

And sometimes, inhaling
springtime from an April
breeze, I catch a glimpse—
what it might be like
to not be me, not succumb
to the fool's gold fantasy my
vision is universal. (Only Laura knows:
my life paint-by-privilege, the seams
of my confidence sewn with ignorance.)

Should I apologize
for these luxuries of advantage?
Is there one among us who
does not project their sight
onto the world? Has there been

a man without a cave
in his heart where raw bankrupt
air makes his bones chatter
and compassion freeze?

When I wear the red
tie, I am only
what I am needed to be:
straight and shiny
below the perfect
knot
that holds me
together.

Relapse

My ex had a vice
in her brain that squeezed the wild expanse of her
shut, demanded she notice pimples,
fat deposits on thighs, her students' low
test scores and how happy she was *that* summer—
the handle of this mental dam spun
clockwise, sealing her
unfettered flow.

I'd rub her calves,
shoulders, kiss her neck, pronounce
the names of world capitals, present
my unconditional adoration to the door-
slamming sentinel in her head.

My father would have said *It's because she's a Virgo*
but that's not the point.

She wanted to drink again
and I understood—anything
to quell the tightfisted sizzle,
each movement and word under scrutiny.

I wanted to tell her the treasure
of her heart would not be lost
to an undertow of betrayal, that
her cheeks were bookends between
which I'd happily read. But I held
my tongue, afraid that neither
logic nor love could tame
the captious watchdog
of her mind.

Mailboxes

The symmetry of mailboxes: bunched
in threes, icicles dangling
from their chins,

in the snow, over a curb, by a street,
in a town—they do not move
but wait to be filled.

Sometimes a handwritten
letter reminds them of human
exchange. More often

than not, their meals are slick,
perfume-inserted, statutory
and digit thick. The life

of a mailbox is lonely, but they
have no choice but to wait and nod at salt and slush
and plow scars with their somber wilting flags.

We do.
We must not wait
to be filled.

Not the Me Myself

Hiking roads free
of grime and motion, in white
gales whipping hubris from my mind,
I felt my soul zip-gone—
to a still point where truth
was laid bare—and the swing
of my arm and certitude
of my boots were but epilogues
of a seamless vanishing. My eyes held
the flannel, shoveling world while I strode
deeper into another, the cold
nudging my distant skin.

I cannot be measured
by my appearance in a house,
in the school where I work
or in photographs on the top shelf
of an office bookcase; the me myself
lends out a body while it soars
over the resplendent floor
of the world, spurred on by euphonic
choirs of troubled hearts and the rich
prospect of egos laid low.

I am but a shadow on location,
living elsewhere in this body, in the attic
of my brain reading books, in the basement
of my heart painting with fingers, or in the hot
air balloon of my soul, landing only to love
or when the beauty is simply too great.

The Leaf Inspector

While toddlers march behind
toy strollers, kick soccer balls
and seek more than hide, you
scan the September playground
for deciduous issue, ululating
at leaves that pirouette
to the black mat
where you sit.

You lean forward, index
and thumb a crane that lifts, crunches
then sprinkles your tiny coat
with a thousand flecks of white oak,
these nascent days of autumn—
summer still at the table
drinking tea, not quite ready
for the drive home.

You comb each leaf of fingered neon
like an Egyptologist, eyes tracking
tributaries to their source,
each vein slanting toward stem—
echoes of a tree from which
all have fallen.

Children scramble like mice,
their screams calling you to attention,
and you crawl, hair blazing, palms
slapping toward slides, moats, castles of bars
where, exuberant, you rest on your left
raise your right
and offer a treasure-filled hand
to mystified eyes.

The line of your brow lifts,
eyes circling lagoons at strangers
whom to you seem so big—
you reach with absolute sincerity
as if to say: *Here is the answer.*

This is union—a bridge between us.
Take it, I found it for you while you were playing.

The children run, made shy
by the brave crawling boy with orange hair
and perfect conviction. You crawl
to the next group, and the next
until all have grown timid
and fled.

Alone, among knobby twigs
and dusty shoe prints, you turn
to me, your father—last hope in the dusk
of Queens playground:

You lean on your left,
raise your right, and stare
straight through to my trunk.
I take your leaf and sweet
hand in mine, catch my breath
and thank you, vein to vein,
for the truth that races through
your lithe, arboreal limbs.

T r u n k
for Rainer and Atticus

Your frames house
the bones of ancestors;
his eyes, her chin, their hair
in faces that radiate
when your mother looks at you
just so.

You are the dirt rooted
to mantel and crust,
eight wellsprings
of immigrant: *Ades, Casale, Fishman, Langbein,
Muuss, Pasca, Petzelt* and *Schwanzer.*

Everything we are
is in you,
two boys: part code,
moment, mitosis, wind
part us, part God
beyond comprehension.

We fumble skillfully
in the face of ignorance. It is the best
we can do, our humility
a forest of reaching
trees, our joy the boughs,
your laughter sylvan,
our future rising
from before these roots
began into the great
unwritten sky.

Closing of a Nation

A sea of white insurance
records floated over Manhattan—
no two perforations alike.
Flights were grounded, borders
closed, ballgames postponed, theme parks
and embassies cleaned out
like spring cupboards.

But this was not a snow day.

After the collapse, Godzillas
of smoke billowed through alleyways,
gnashed at downtown limbs and shoeless
feet with jaws of soot and shards
of what were once windows
on the world.

Professionals plunged from the sky,
choosing flight over caldrons of faxes
aflame with jet fuel. Charred shoes settled
between rooftop vents while stunned figures inched
across an ashen bridge—a modern Trail of Tears—
fleeing *The Capital of the Civilized World*
on foot.

We were sent home from school,
but this was not a snow day.

Teeming cancellations scrolled
in gold across black bottoms of American
TVs; the Towers blew down
and we feel pain in places we didn't know
our patriotism ran.

And I sense today what a veteran knows:
ease forever pierced by that imminent
needle of danger. As firefighters vanished
beneath rubble and glass, hoses rent, our hearts
burning, CBS, NBC, ABC and CNN

closed around this nightmare
like the clenched throbbing fingers of a fist.

Our president said:
We will hunt down and find those folks.
But *folks* run general stores and bingo halls;
folks don't carve through skyscrapers;
folks don't shatter the cadence
of earthly affairs.

Before America closed,
there was a fire drill at my school—
8:15am, thirty minutes before time cracked.
My secretary friends joked they'd burn
with the building when I asked if they were coming.
Our nonchalant march to the great lawn, teachers
propping dark industrial doors, administrators crossing
walkie-talkies to sunlit ears—
it wasn't a real fire, but it could have been;
today everywhere is ground zero.

Still, we cannot half-live
from headline to hazard;
the record of human strength is too
thick, the opportunity too precious
to bungle as we approach a day
when all heads of state will recognize
what is so clear from a distance.

But tonight, in this warm September gloom,
phone calls made, eyes swollen and TV dumb,
as cabbies rip back seats out for dead
bodies en route to makeshift morgues, I find myself wishing
for a snow day.

Dead of Winter

Persephone sprawls on Hades' throne, picking
pomegranate seeds from her teeth, knowing
it doesn't matter anymore what she eats: bride
of the underworld till spring.

(Her white sundress hangs in a walk-in
crypt by the lush vale of Enna where she was
plucked, and where her basket of hyacinth
remains—stiff and still as a headstone).

She speaks to the recent dead, droll
anecdotes—her husband's woeful self-pity,
Charon's coin collection and the shortcut to Styx
she found playing hide and seek with Cerberus. But
when the audience of shades slips home, Persephone
paces unseen through catacombs, reading
her mother's letters and weeping.

This morning, as a coin of food clanked
off the floor of my stomach, and the auger
of February school bells, ticking vents and split
skin tunneled chill through my heart, I remembered
the Goddess confined: we, too, are wed
to darkness, rising each day under changeless
skies—a single black robe stretched like a bridge
from end of winter to the other.

Or maybe we are Demeter: grieving
mothers steeling ourselves against the graying
of the world, experience all that buoys
us through bleak quarters of calendars—for birth
is more tenacious than death, and our gloom,
like the seasons, is fleeting.

And soon Demeter will set her table
for two, expecting Persephone's red-lipped
hello to poke through the frosted
ground and bloom in green
twitching dashes.

Definitions of a Baseball

The seed
that fertilizes
spring, impregnates
the air with a whirring
tumbling joy; the pill
that skids toward
an unwieldy boy, stiff mitt,
outstretched leather
below his waist,
precarious and hopeful;
the orb that disappears
in the turning dusk
of pebbled cleats,
motley grass, earthen
squish, fading lime;
the sphere that hangs
in sepia snapshots
of banjos and barnstorming,
around which summer blooms
and lives ramify
like the roots of this
red-stitched seed.

White Boys of Summer

They know someday they'll be
called *boss*, sign off on payroll, flirt
with their secretaries and carry
each other's business cards
in sleek sterling cases.

This spring their skin is not
entirely white, salon-tanned for some
freckled for others, though they are born
knowing who's in charge. And so
they trash strangers' dens, hoodwink
teachers, degrade lunch ladies, cheat
on girls and exams and humiliate their own
friends—no one safe from the snickering
of their adolescence—because they must enjoy
the full extent of their rights.

Anything that makes a good Friday night
story with the guys—slapping knees over red
plastic cups and a keg that never runs dry—
is worth doing.

People say money corrupts
but it's *how* it's passed down
tells boys whose bootstraps will never need pulling
it's okay to flip off the mom on her porch
across the street from home plate, then
trawl Third Avenue in a convertible,
stretching the legs of their immunity.

The white boys of summer decide
who is worthy and who
is not, though they wouldn't know
the difference if it cracked them
in the face with
a 30-ounce
Scandium Alloy
Z-core
Easton
ConneXion.

Pumps

Isn't it time we admit
Cinderella's slipper never did fit?

Painted toes crammed—
a pregnant stomach and spleen—
crushed leather knob at the tip
where five wiggly piggies wee-wee-weed
to market for heels that cinch
their pedicured heads like a noose,
Jimmy Choos kicked
off minutes into the party
to unseal the foot
like a vacuum-packed can of Cheetos.

Or crack a checkbook, dish
out two-grand for a surgeon
who will slice divinely
disfigured digits and score
a jacuzzi with the profit—
China's legacy alive and well:
shoes that bind
tendons, mangle women's
feet to petite camel humps
while men
change comfortably
from Nikes to sandals to boots—
the wide landscape of their feet preserved
like National Parks.

Blue Sign, Route 30

West of Gettysburg, cornflower ink drying in National Park passports,
we are shared apples, car-seat crayons, I-spy guessing and wide-eyed
gaping at mountains under mist, the Tuscarora rising over
homes of quarried stone; an historical marker by the street—
blue metal, gold chevrons on its shoulders like a general—
reads NELLIE FOX HOUSE.

And I am in my parents' bedroom, a '59 Nellie Fox
in my ten-year-old palm, tangerine oval framing his face,
Hall of Fame fingers poised to pensive chin, as if
ready to catch his own voice.

My father's baritone barrels like a ground ball
down the line, fingers hooked with disease, yellowed
with smoke and snot as they sort Bowman and Goudey, ashes spilling
onto bed sheets, nine-pocket plastic and baseball cards between us.
He recalls Polo Grounds doubleheaders and claims Juan Samuel
is a sure bet for the Hall—a step above, say, Nellie Fox.

I am mute while we search without
purpose through stacks of thin rectangular stock.
The dark truth of a baseball card—it's always a year behind:
Chicago in cursive over the snapshot of a pitcher now
with Houston, his lifetime E.R.A. of 3.71 inflated by May
to 3.85, weight now 217 after a series near his favorite
Philly cheesesteak joint.

My father, blood-sugar spiked, slouching in jean shorts
and white v-neck that hangs—a cotton chain—from his waning
body, is hoping to know me. This ritual of grins
and proclamations renders the day interminable, though evening
is worse. He limps late to the table, police line-up
of pills, wondering which one will make him wretch
till his bitterness comes out with the bile.

Moisture still glistening on his nostril, he trashes the food—
two pounds down on his card—then picks a fight with his eldest;
so ill, proud and young, my father squanders his best resource:
two admiring sons, a devoted wife—none of us enough.

Long before he died on a cold November morning,
my mother had lost a spouse, Jesse and I
our parents and the chance to be brothers.
Did he not know of others' struggles? Had he
not scanned the backs of cards passed between us
so many stale afternoons? Hall of Famers fail
two-thirds of the time. Even Nellie Fox struck out.

Behind the wheel on Route 30, St. Thomas, PA,
beneath the mist and grandeur of mountains,
these memories conjure the thrum of an old sprain,
whistle of an empty tooth I might once have felt—
no more now than numbers on the back of a card
or a blue sign with gold chevrons by the road.

THANKING THE BUDDHA

Wash

My son
is not tall enough
to reach the sink
his voice wispy
airborne like spring spiders
says *daddy*
wash hands?
I spin
the brass
fixture lift
his snow-white
arms to
the basin
he smiles
the water
surges a luminous
beam of wanting of cleansing
my love for him
a faucet
even I
can't
shut
off.

Remnants

An Andes candy exposed on the top
ledge of the fridge, its silver leaf ticking
the temperature gauge, triangles of abandoned
pizza, naked pots of soup, browning lettuce,
half-sliced yams littering the shelves
with good intentions.

Third of unpeeled banana stuck face
down to the rim of clay purple dish on
snack tray, swirls of chocolate hair wound
about the mouth of the drain, a five-foot
mirror propped seventy-five degrees against the bedroom
wall, Bobbi Brown kit at its base.

Nomadic CDs dashed across the pine-stained
bureau, holey grey panties at the foot
of the mattress, scraps of scalloped fabric
on the sunroom floor left illumined,
again, by a neglected switch.

These remains—signposts of your movement
through rooms—were a map I followed
to track down the treasure of intimacy.

My memory, now, is a hollow chest,
your words sea-green morsels of glass,
fear the kelp choking our shared secret:

that we were not meant for each other—
our years never sealed properly, their
expiration date a stamp we
were too scared to read.

Half-Mast

Sunday, June 5th, 2004: eight children and fourteen grandchildren mourn in
London, Boston and Nakuru, remembering Teresia Watiri Mutuura.

Imagine your stomach said
to your heart, your brain, or the red vault
of your throat, *Enough! I hereby declare*
my independence! then ceded from your
corporeal union, boxing off in pastels
like Ohio and Nebraska, Egypt and Turkey—
each district of you choosing for a flag
its own patriotic helix.

They strain to recall Mwariki Farm and the gleam of Teresia's agate smile in
coffee beans, polished rosewood and still water.

Any fool knows the supple chunks
of you can't go it alone—every gear
set in motion by the others, like a watch,
the weather, the planets winging just so
around the sun.

Ms. Mutuura passed at age 66 while gazing at the chiseled treetops below
her Nairobi Hospital window. She had transferred from MCF Ward just for
the view.

Somehow, we fail to apply this simple anatomy
to the body of our world; organs spurn
cellular bonds and synaptic liaisons, muscle
shuns bone and limbs are annexed by rogue
electric pulses. The heart beats for whomever
it wants when its own interests are at stake.
Until one of *us* is struck down. Then
we mouth somber prayers at half-mast
by the bleak tinging of rope against pole.

On three continents, Teresia's descendants embrace, thank God and take
aimless nourishing walks past storefronts and headlines that blare RONALD
REAGAN DEAD AT 93.

Five-Cent Poem

It just so happens
I am tired of trudging in
salt-stained shoes to the corner
market, a bowling bag slung
around my wrist, crammed
with soda cans.

It so happens I am tired
of doing this deed—
parading my icy bones
over curbs mottled
with foam, foil
and gym shorts stitched with tire tracks.

I am tired
of lurching through lentic
pools of week-old water,
around buses plastered
with neon, just to arrive
at the dank malodorous door
of Refund.

I am tired and blood-blushed
with wind and sweat, pinching
planet-pleasing nickels.

Robert Moses Field Two, 1983

Rusted trash cans dot the noble
coast between boardwalk bottles
and an ocean gagged by FM
radio and Boeing reverb.

A blond, coil-haired scholar near
the misty hiss of Atlantic shoreline reads
at his blanket, hindered by the wind-muted cries
of a child with a soiled suit; he shakes
his head to chase dancing spots
from his eyelids, then stops for advertisements in the sky
and neon bikinis tracing tanned thighs and
breasts globing out into the sun.

Three gulls dart for an apple core, two
state employees wear lawnmower-green
sleeves cut off—Historic Preservation stitched
in white around the nipple—snip Ssips and Hostess
boxes with cheap metal pinchers and a boy
and girl of nineteen share a Michelob.

At umbrella row, a fur-bellied
father laughs, spits cherry
pits, crimson stones dyeing
the flesh of the sand, his son—
stiff sapphire shorts stenciled white
along the seams—lost in the calm
assurance of shovel in, shovel out, shovel in,
shovel out, his mother smacking shadows
of horseflies after they've struck.

The Egyptian Collection

Dendur now sits in a sunny high-ceilinged room, sequestered
by rope and reflecting pool—terrace chipped, scarabs still,
papyrus reaching for the Nile and Africa.

The Thursday afternoon crush points, clicks and murmurs
about the *When Harry Met Sally* pecan pie scene, shot
between Ra's nightly battle with Apep and the dappled
windows beveled towards Central Park.

Earth is restless where I sit, on a flush ecru wall above the pool; it remembers
Dendur, in Lower Nubia: empire of gates and temples of sandstone, winged
stone, scarab stone, alchemist beetles turning dung into gold. Dynasties made
gold, conquerors made gold, companies made gold hustling Nubian stone—
a realm left to smolder like a derelict house.

I can no more restore these eight hundred tons
to their naked tract of earth south of Aswan
than move zoo giraffes back to the savannah. Instead I write
in a green journal about cushioned feet circling Dendur's shallow moat,
combed daily by men in goggles, jumpsuits and African skin.

The museum-goers stop to make wishes, then toss
their gold in the water.

Antalya

Yellow hair—caught
in Mediterranean spindrift—
wet tendrils splayed
down your tilted neck,
crimson bikini framing
piston arms and tight clover
of cleavage, pale
against the sea.

Your body knew nothing, then
of exhaustion—
of years spent
in hushed starlight, nursing
babies towards sleep,
into sleep, back to sleep, after sleep:

of squatting down, picking up,
boiling rice, icing bumps,
rocking, singing, teaching—
deciding like breathing.

On that Turkish beach, your skirt
flapped from your silhouette
the way lovers loosen
on honeymoon. Four years

later,
in the quarter moon
of our bedroom,
I trail my cheek through your quiet hair
and stare down exhaustion till it shines.

Our legs straddle
two continents:
hands tangled, lips pressed
across epochs, our love more fierce
than empires that crumbled and left
only aqueducts and prosceniums.

For the Taliban

We in the modern world envy you
because we do not have time
to do what we want. You uncover secrets
no physicist could fathom: skipping Earth's orbit
while we breathe through contractions
of change. You expand by shrinking
horizons of the mind—mushroom flash
turning justice and liberty to sand.

You have all day to make
sure no one in Kabul plays
the trumpet, cards or chess, or screens
a film. At your leisure, you can ensure
all non-Muslims are wearing their Yellow Stripe,
that your shrouded women (allowed to bake bread
the way our inmates produce license plates)
aren't getting uppity, aren't pointing
out that you are stuck in
an oven of myopia.

Even Mother Nature, for whom nothing
is stagnant, has fled Afghanistan; you have cut
millennia down at the knees, forged a reign of anachronism
where death by stoning is in vogue, and females—
once judges, teachers and authors of your
constitution—are barred from pen and page.

You hand guns to starving boys
and survey the demolition of a Buddha, high
above the cliffs of Bamiyan where it has stood
since the days of Muhammad, whose Islam
you drag through the dust.

O Taliban, your world may be timeless
but not immortal; the *hijabs* and *niqaabs*
which veil the promise of your nation
will open soon enough.

The Mathematics of Letting Go

I am a puppy tracing timid
zig-zags across a field, gauging
the air, barely aware the broad
swale of green is mine
for the taking.

I wait for the other shoe
to drop on this blessing
of arms, gift of lips, windfall
of words that swirl a G-clef,
a figure eight between us.
But the sweetness doesn't
cloy like that final niblet of candy
corn, mulching fructose in waves
of bruised orange.

My surprise resonates
instead, in soaring arcs
and exponents, love multiplying
in permutations I can shout!
or keep to myself
and either way, know this
is the most
immeasurable thing
I have known.

At Knollwood

Freckles filtered sunlight
enough to dust her skin with summer corn,
birds lounging in her childhood
spruce, cats curling in her old
playhouse and juice crackling
in a plastic cup while the protractor
of her mind measured the angles
between things: birdfeeders, clouds, power lines,
clothespins and the gyrating pool—
her gaze the hypotenuse
bisecting past and present, her heart—
addled by modern confusions
and sanctified memories—
calls hoarsely from the obtuse
junction of her body,
burning in degrees
of acute August sun.

Toll

Smog accumulates loved ones
in our lungs blackening air laced
with carcinogens yet
when the sun from Montauk crests
tree lines beneath the Whitestone Bridge—
cirrus catching pink plumes of sherbet gilt
lavender more dramatic than museum paintings—
we see that pain has made us
spectacular.

The Listmaker

In the hole of afternoon between school and family
when dust loops in shafts above my bed, I want nothing
but a reference book, pen and pad.

Heading 1: Animal
Heading 2: Weight
Heading 3: Gestation Period

Light from the window gone, the house
has changed—holes filled with meals
and resentments.

Heading 1: Father
Heading 2: Brother
Heading 3: Mother

I hold my breath across awkward lanes
of impact, ships butting bows, cleaving rudders
till I sweep back to books.

Heading 1: Planet
Heading 2: Moon(s)
Heading 3: Distance From the Sun

Or country, population and hospital beds per 1,000,
my classmates by row and desk, my top 100 songs,
states I want to visit or friends I wish I had.

Lists of lists, as if headings
and columns are pillars
holding what might fall
down and disappear:
lists are obvious,
lists are safe,
lists include or do not
without complication.

Long Poems

I.
I've always been envious of long poems—
how with verses like blades of grass
and Roman I's and V's they
build and protract.

II.
I can't write poems like that.

III.
I thought poetry was a distillation
of truths to their essence—
like sifting through formulas
equations and calculations
for that single
rigid
beatific
numeral.

To My One-Month-Old

When I peer over the rim
of bassinette, your limbs whirl like summer
pinwheels, torso a still pink stick.

Your eyes shift wide and blue
from ceiling to blinds to the painting above the couch;
you study, while nursing,
the contrast of light and dark,
jagged and smooth,
as if aware that when the fertile body
of your mother pulls away
the world steps in.

Like colostrum, this planet
provides all we need, so long
as we array ourselves in
the raiment of wonder.

For now, go on smiling when you pass gas;
kicking the piston of your right leg like a drummer;
chopping down at mommy's chest with your wild
left arm as if slashing a path through Amazon brush;
and casting your breath into the briny years between us.

Where I'm From

I am from the four-year prayer
of a poet and his wife,
an artist and her husband,
from brewer's yeast and tiger's milk,
kindness and peace.

I am from doorway Alla'u'abhas
and bear-hugging strangers in dens dimly
lit, from felt banners and folding chair
basements where song and scripture
soothed the din of rankled babies.
I am from Fireside refreshments: platters
of saffron pilaf, blueberry cheese tarts, apple
wedges and sliced cheddar. I am from Pouran and Amir,
Carlos and Hong, Siapoosh and Muzhan in neat
semi-circles—one planet, one people, please.

I am from the Psychic Game, Ouija Board and Zodiac divination,
from the four-dimensional cognizance
of a pin oak leaf idly rocking.

I am from *that* house
without cable, VCR and microwave,
from surfeit bookshelves, PBS telethons
Phil Ochs and family trips in a blue mildewed Maverick
to abandoned New England quarries—
I am from beryl and tourmaline, garnet and quartz,
from hammering until palms callused
and blistered; I am from green grapes
and PB&Js in the sun.

I am from an island shaped like a fish,
a township sealed and split by ethnicity
like the quadrants of a frozen TV dinner—
my section stuffed like a three-day
suitcase with second generation Italians.
I am from the profoundly saddening
alienating realization that my home
and hometown were nothing alike—(Take Exit 38

off Sunrise Highway, turn right at Terrace Diner—
I am from just over the bridge).

I am from atlases, almanacs and scribing recondite
lists with the fastidiousness of a savant.
I am, I yam, Iamb from puns and repuns-el let down your hair.
I am from crisp autumn leaf mounds,
pristine winter forts and setting wet gloves
over an orange kerosene dome till they stiffened.

I am from my father's diabetes, dextrose and insulin,
his coarse jokes and wads of sugarless gum tossed
nightly at Kaity Tong while she anchored the six o'clock news.
I am from fetching sweaters, Hershey squares, spiral
notebooks and a pot for him to piss in.
I am from the dank orange room at the end of the hall
where his blood swirled like V8 Juice through circus straws.

I am from the lash of his regret,
the ignition of my brother's rage
and the spoon-clank echo of my mother's sacrifice.
I am from cradling my cat in the mute forgotten corner of a family.
I am from the flax wind-blown reeds of my father's funeral.
I am from growing old before I was young.

I am from Moscow trams, hikes to glaciers,
Bryce hoodoos and release.
I am from *Far Above Cayuga's Waters*
where gorges mended the cracks
in my soul, and words, film
and freedom launched me
into mesosphere. I am from the lie
of a beginning, a middle and an end.

I am from breathless epiphany
and the lucid certainty that
I am from you,
you are from me
and that we, together,
are merely from
the illusion of a difference.

Satellite

I plunge my right shoe into black
slush, unslit my lids with streetlight,
prop the ridge of my skull against
the smeared glass of a ten-car train,
its red, digitized conductor and two-note
door chime sweeping in the frost—
one station to the next, day
after day, ticket bare
in my languid hand.

I am in orbit
around wife and son
who spin in place—a planet
of tickles and fingerpaint.

Between commutes, I work
joyfully, while grieving that we three
meet only in confused
moments of sky. My prolific motion
craves anchoring; her indefatigable
crafting of home craves rambling.
Our celestial dance is the gravity
of parenthood.

Commencement

We ponder siblings who trick, parents
who can't let go, why Iago torments The Moor
and how to balance between Happy and Biff.

We confront our inner monsters, grasp
talismans as we pluck forward, string words
together that pull our pasts into view and laugh
at our shameful imperfections.

We share weekend escapades, observations
about the moon, pangs of rejection and failure
and run-ins with the machinery of expectation.

We long together for the sacred ground
Seattle spoke of and the Goddess who once nourished us all—
we ask our most dangerous questions.

We are in tears, in love, in distress, in abeyance
for nine months: a classroom, a womb
where thoughts contract,
breaking silence, bringing courage closer
and closer to light.

When the crowds arrive on a hot sudden night at the end
of June, the water breaks, and it's white
folding chairs on football sidelines, trellised platforms
where the big wigs sit and parents doused
in jewelry and cologne grin snapshots and call for reservations.
Every year I watch them go—
then drive home.

By the moonlit jetty of midnight,
waves ramming rocks in palpitations,
my heart glimmers across the water of the bay—
too far to swim, too near to ignore.

Were it the swiveling torch of a lighthouse
I would take a quicker route, to bridge this
awkward passage between blessings.

Certain Voyage

My wife is the best kind
of predictable—
bone wrists whip
to bend and swoosh,
diction balmy, heart
fervent, attention keen
to the ripping seam
of minutes. These
are things to count on.
I form no gambit
when we meet—
no method to undulate
through conversations.

Our days are halcyon:
the snowbank of her
neck melts down
the slope of her
chest into a bosom
of sun-cooled miles.
I press my cheek
to her in all conditions
and places—
sailing around the world:
a Magellan of her skin.

The Peconic

Today I am Corchaug in a silver Grumman canoe, sidling along
a cranberry bog that dyed red the mouths of Pilgrims.

J-strokes straighten my bow through raining locks of willow, knotted
arbors of wood, banks untouched but for a sliver
of sun where dragonflies mate like snared knuckles.

Placing paddle on knees, I stop to float—
head thrown back, I swallow the Paumanok sky, filling my lungs
and limbs with a timeless maternal peace.

At Connecticut Ave., I have to step out of the canoe, hoist
its length over lane paint and oil stains, losing sight
in cobwebs beneath the expressway. Further upstream,

in browning water, I collide with a couch, its dangling arm about to shade
a sunning turtle, my oar grazing mailbox flags and beer cans, soda tabs
and dark droves of boat scraps trolling the riverbed like Kevlar stingrays.

Past haggard backs of dealerships, bait and tackle stands,
ice cream shops—veins in my shoulders stinging with fatigue—
my Corchaug dream bows in submission.

In the rental shop lot, I turn in my gear, hose the strain and slime
from my skin and stand: silent and weary, ashamed
of what it means, today, to be native.

Racing Toothpicks

When it rains, part of me
wants to crouch over a white curb
whose pebbles bubble out like blisters,
crouch so low my shorts scrape
the dewy heads of dandelions. One foot
astride the current, one on the stripe
of sidewalk grass, toothpicks in
my eight-year-old hand. The day
slows, then stops, so that it will always
be me, the storm and adventure.
Flow forged by road pitch
and sewer grate, the torrent speeds
in ribbed v's over my hunching
silhouette. I drop a toothpick—it sticks
to a reef of gummed weeds
then shoots into necklines of rippling
runoff. Streamlined steamer, this missile
made for picking teeth, stabbing
sandwiches or tearing through the black
rushing tide at curbside. It rains harder,
so hard it runs into my eyes, gusts across
my stooped body, sealing forever
my skin beneath the tight clear
saran wrap of my shirt.

When Joy Breaks

When joy breaks
like the purling rills of spring,
laughter spiraling through tiny windows,
a dolphin slapping its cold blue back
against the sea;

When joy breaks
and spins free the spigots of my mind,
I want to stay awake for the rest
of my life—

Seeking glad conspiracies
of atoms,
the wax seals
of God's greatest love notes:
each breath
a yearning,
each day
a crown of elms,
each story
a breeze soothing our lonesome crags,
each sorrow
a luminous jolt of flight.

And when it's all over
I hope to say:

This life made of me a lantern,
a whitish beacon of matter
staining the sky
long after my cells
had scattered.

AcKNoWLedgeMeNtS & THaNKS

Grateful acknowledgment is made to the following publications in which these poems appeared, sometimes in slightly different forms.

The Long Island Quarterly, Autumn 2001: "March Baseball"
The Pedestal Magazine (www.thepedestalmagazine.com): "Closing of a Nation"
Stillwater Magazine (www.JB Stillwater.com): "When Joy Breaks" and "Grace"

Much of the work in this book was written over the span of a decade, though not until recently has enough time and organization presented itself for the actual assemblage of a manuscript. That task, as anyone knows who has undertaken it, is enormously tedious and humbling. Here I offer my thanks to those who made that task bearable and, hopefully, successful: Susan Barbash, Sammy Caiola, Laura Diamond, David Dopko, Ellen Fishman, Leslie Gurowitz Harris, Jim Hopkins, Rachel Kaufman, Laura Iacobucci Lima, Candace McClellan, Lisa Ober, Shannon O'Donovan, Jose Ramirez, Athena Reich, Daniel Rigazzi, Lawrence Rush, Jeannette Senneca, Sriram Shankar, Dan Sullivan, Paul Trapani, Lillian Udell, Megan Vitols-McKay, Michelle White and Jenna Young.

In addition, I am forever indebted to the professional feedback freely offered by Druzelle Cederquist, Kyle G. Dargan, Charles Fishman, Veronica Golos and Alan Semerdjian.

I offer special thanks to Nicole Galante and Jennifer Reilly Magliano for their ebullient and proactive support, Jon Link for being both the first person to take an interest in my writing and a role model when I sorely needed one, Jon Nelson for keeping me tethered to writing during difficult times, Nina Wolff for her consummate devotion to art, education and her "Englishers", even after retirement, Jesse Pasca for his encouragement and brilliant cover art, Janet Brennan for her generosity and belief in my work, Harriet Pasca-Ortgies for her unconditional love and faith, and my boys, Atticus and Rainer, for sharpening my sight and heart every day.

To all you amazing souls who comprise the vast network of loving, creative and supportive people in my life—students, teachers, cousins, aunts, uncles and friends alike—this book is an outgrowth of my experience, of which you have all been integral parts.

Lastly, I would like to thank Terri Muuss, who has now spent as much time with these poems as I have, and is the best editor, partner, wife, co-parent and friend a guy could find.

Notes

A Thousand Doors: Excerpted and summarized from *Kindness: A Treasury of Buddhist Wisdom for Children and Parents.* Collected and adapted by Sarah Conover, Eastern Washington University Press, Spokane, WA, 2001.

E-Train Blues: Emulation of Soul Coughing's *Screenwriter's Blues,* from their album *Ruby Vroom,* Slash Records, Los Angeles, CA, 1994.

Tanyou: The Chinese "Tanyou" translates to "In Search of Quietude", according to a plaque in Astor Court on the second floor of the Metropolitan Museum of Art in New York City, where its symbol hangs over a door. "Nataraj" is the name of the Hindu God Shiva when Lord of the Dance of creation and destruction.

The Oldest Story: According to many, *The Epic of Gilgamesh* is Earth's oldest extant story. It was written on twelve clay tablets in cuneiform script in Ancient Sumeria.

In Lieu of Narnia: Title and references throughout the poem allude to C.S. Lewis's series of books entitled *The Chronicles of Narnia,* Harper Collins, UK, 1950-1956.

Letters: Emulation of *Numbers* by Mary Cornish, from *Red Studio,* Oberlin College Press, Oberlin, OH, 2007.

This Week Had Arms: The Russian phrase in the last stanza means "Because I love her".

Perigee: Astronomical term for the point in a satellite's orbit closest to the object being orbited.

Redshift: Astronomical phenomenon in which a source of light moving away from its observer appears red, due to the stretching of its wavelengths.

Feet: Emulation of *Hairs* by Sandra Cisneros, from *House on Mango Street,* Arte Publico Press, Houston, TX, 1984.

Gateau de Mille-Feuilles (Cake of a Thousand Leaves): Original French term, and its translation, for a Napoleon pastry.

For Remus Lupin: In J.K. Rowlings' *Harry Potter* series, published by Bloomsbury, UK, 1997-2007, Remus Lupin is a Professor at Hogwarts School of Witchcraft and Wizardry. He is a werewolf who must vigilantly take medicine and/or steer clear of full moons in order to remain his good-natured, positive and connected self. A Patronus is an advanced charm cast by savvy wizards and witches to fend off Dementors—indifferent suckers of souls. A Patronus must be cast from a place of utter innocence and joy.

Osiris Speaks to Isis: In the Egyptian myth, Osiris's villainous brother Set, God of the Desert, kills Osiris, God of Vegetation. The Goddess Isis, Osiris's wife, makes an epic search for her husband's body and resurrects him with her powers.

A Thank You to William Bayard Cutting: The Bayard Cutting Arboretum is a state park on the south shore of Long Island in Great River, NY.

Mako Sica: The Lakotan "Mako Sica" translates to "Badlands" or "Difficult Place to Cross."

Dead of Winter: In the Greek myth, innocent and vibrant Persephone is abducted by Hades, God of the Underworld, and confined there. A deal is ultimately brokered so that Persephone only spends one-third of the year in Tartarus. Demeter, Persephone's mother and Goddess of the Harvest and Agriculture, became known for withdrawing her powers of fertility during her daughter's absence—an early explanation for seasons.

Wash: This was written during a workshop with Naomi Shihab Nye at Bay Shore High School's nationally-recognized annual Ethnic Pen conference for young writers.

Half-Mast: Italicized portion of this poem inspired by an obituary found on line at *www.misterseed.com/ORBITUARIES/ORBITUARIESmay2004.htm*

Five-Cent Poem: Inspired by Pablo Neruda's *Walking Around,* from *Neruda and Vallejo: Selected Poems,* Beacon Press, Boston, MA, 1993.

The Egyptian Collection: The Temple of Dendur is the crown jewel of the Metropolitan Museum of Art's Egyptian collection in New York City. A Nubian temple built in Egypt around 15BC, Dendur was gifted to the USA in 1965 in order to save it from destruction, due to the construction of the Aswan High Dam. Depictions of the nightly battle between the sun God, Ra, and the villainous serpent of the Underworld, Apep, appear on a large sarcophagus in this room.

For the Taliban: Written, strangely, on September 6th, 2001.

Where I'm From: Emulation of George Ella Lyon's *Where I'm From,* from *Where I'm From: Where Poems Come From,* Absey and Co. Spring, TX. 1999. "Alla'u'abha" is Arabic for "God the All-Glorious" and is a common Baha'i greeting. A "Fireside" is an informal Baha'i gathering whose goal is the fostering of spiritual community and theological/philosophical discussion. *Far Above Cayuga's Waters*—Cornell University's Alma Mater—was written in 1870 by roommates Archibald Croswell Weeks and Wilmot Moses Smith. "Pin oak leaf, idly rocking" is from Robert Pasca's *Lamentation at the End of the Wind,* from *Directions to My House,* Nine Points Press, Babylon, NY, 1982.

Commencement: Iago is the infamous villain of Shakespeare's *Othello,* Happy and Biff are Willy Loman's two sons in *Death of a Salesman* and Seattle is the Anglicized spelling of the Indian chief Sealth from the Pacific Northwest, famous for his remarks about his people's intimate relationship to the land and the white man's disdain for that land.

The Peconic: The Corchaug were one of the many Indian tribes that for centuries, if not millennia, inhabited the region now called Long Island. "Paumanok" is the native name for Long Island. It means "Land of Tribute".

When Joy Breaks: Emulation of *When Death Comes* by Mary Oliver, from *New and Selected Poems,* Beacon Press, Boston, MA, 1993.

About the Author

Matt Pasca makes his home on the south shore of Long Island in Bay Shore, New York with his wife Terri and sons Rainer and Atticus. A graduate of Cornell University and Stony Brook University, he has taught Creative Writing, Mythology and Literature at Bay Shore High School since 1997. He was named New York State Teacher of Excellence in 2003 and is the adviser of *The Writers' Block,* named Most Outstanding High School Literary-Art Magazine for 2010 by the American Scholastic Press Association. This is Pasca's first full-length manuscript. For bookings and inquiries, contact Matt at simileman@optonline.net.

About the Artist

Jesse Pasca is an artist and educator who splits his time between New York City and Sag Harbor, New York. He richly enjoys urban and rural velocities and his work and life are committed to creating new "circuitry", both individually and as part of larger communities. To view projects and learn more about Jesse and his work, visit www.jpasca.com.

Also By JBStillwater Publishing

Visit us at http://www.jbstillwater.com or http://www.casadesnapdragon.com for information on these and many other fine books

Dark Salt: A Brush With Genius
Lynn Strongin
ISBN 978-0-9845681-4-7

Available in paperback and eBook

In this collection of late works by Lynn Strongin, we find that perfect balance of salt and water spiced with symbolism and metaphor that poet Strongin does so well. Jewish Temple offerings included salt and Jews still dip their bread in salt on the Sabbath as a remembrance of those sacrifices.

Reader Notes

Made in the USA
Charleston, SC
03 May 2013